April 15, 2014

D0602034

CAREERS IN COMPUTER TECHNOLOGY™

CAREERS IN
Network
Engineering

To my grandparents Sol and Frances Engelhard, for always being there

Published in 2011 by The Rosen Publishing Group, Inc.
29 East 21st Street, New York, NY 10010

Copyright © 2011 by The Rosen Publishing Group, Inc.

First Edition

Library of Congress Cataloging-in-Publication Data

Grayson, Robert, 1951–
Careers in network engineering/Robert Grayson. — 1st ed.
    p. cm. — (Careers in computer technology)
Includes bibliographical references and index.
ISBN 978-1-4488-1313-1 (library binding)
1. Computer networks—Vocational guidance—Juvenile literature. I. Title.
TK5102.6.G73 2011
004.6023–dc22

2010011090

Manufactured in the United States of America

CPSIA Compliance Information: Batch #W11YA: For further information, contact Rosen Publishing, New York, New York, at 1-800-237-9932.

On the cover: As businesses become increasingly reliant on networks, more jobs in network engineering are becoming available.

Contents

Computer networks are everywhere in today's world, used by corporations and small businesses, government agencies, nonprofit organizations, school systems, hospitals, and the military. These networks are designed to enable people to communicate with each other safely and securely so that they can conduct business, do research, and exchange information.

For these networks to operate efficiently, they need to be constructed, monitored, maintained, upgraded regularly, and kept secure from intruders. This is the job of the network engineer. How critical is the position of network engineer? If the network breaks down in the middle of the night, it is the network engineer who will get the frantic call to fix it immediately.

One of the fastest-growing job sectors in the information technology field, network engineering offers limitless opportunities for people with technical expertise, a flair for problem solving, a keen desire to keep up-to-date on the latest advancements in the field, and a strong commitment to making the network that they are building and maintaining the fastest and most convenient to use. They also must be able to work well under pressure. When things go awry with a network, it can cost companies a lot of money until network functioning is fully restored.

In the time it takes to read this book, a new piece of software to strengthen existing computer networks could be created and released. As a result, network engineers never stop learning.

In addition, the network engineer must act as a liaison between the technical staff and the nontechnical staff. He or she must translate the needs of the organization's managers and other employees into technical language and then communicate in plain English the benefits of the network to the nontechnical staff. This is similar to translating terms from one language to another because most nontechnical employees are baffled by the terms that network engineers use.

Network engineering requires creativity, too, because each organization has its own needs when it comes to access, security, and troubleshooting. Network engineers have to analyze problems, figure out what the organization needs, and then design the network to meet those needs in a way that is fast and easy for everyone to use.

For instance, a large government agency like the Library of Congress might have many layers of access, some guarded by firewalls put in place by network engineers. The Library of Congress' network has a Web site that is open to the public, with Webcasts from the library, news about the library, a history feature, library catalogs, and other public information. The computer network also allows for library employees to communicate with each other and their supervisors without the public gaining access to these internal communications and files.

Because network engineers design and construct these networks and know the passwords to get into every layer of the networks, they must be highly ethical individuals. They are entrusted with access to this often-confidential information, and they cannot violate that trust.

Network engineers are in great demand, and as computers become even more integral to modern life, the field of network engineering promises to offer high-paying jobs for years to come. Squarely at the epicenter of information technology, network engineers play a vital role in the success or failure of a twenty-first-century enterprise.

CHAPTER ① Networks in Today's World

The world is increasingly interconnected, with people constantly looking for new ways to use computer networks and the computer industry responding with ever-faster and better technology. Network engineers, those responsible for forging these connections, are expected to keep up with rapid-fire changes in the field and implement them as soon as they hit the marketplace.

THE NEED FOR NETWORK ENGINEERS

At the moment, there simply are not enough well-trained network engineers to handle the demand, and more are needed all the time. As word gets out about what networks can do to revolutionize fields like law enforcement, government, health care, and education, professionals working in those areas are demanding the latest networking technology.

When news breaks about what one segment of the business world is doing to propel itself into the future, networking is almost always part of the discussion. Health care, for instance, is struggling to come up with ways to enable the top medical minds in far-flung parts of the country to collaborate on a patient's care without having to move that patient from one facility to another and with physicians having access to the patient's records so that they can evaluate the

Computer networks help people in countless ways. At VictimPower. org, network engineers monitor a system that allows victims of sexual abuse to report crimes anonymously.

case simultaneously. How to do this? Networks. While highly skilled physicians are working together to save a life, network engineers at the cutting edge of technology are pooling their talents to provide those doctors with the vital technological tools they need to make that happen.

Networks are not a footnote to what is going on in today's world; they are central to it. In the future, just about every enterprise will rely on networks, and right now the concern is this: will there be enough network engineers to fill the demand?

When the question arises about how to drive a business to the next level, the answer is networks. That means network engineering is where the jobs are.

MAKING AN IMPACT

As the Internet swept through the world in the 1990s, businesses large and small—as well as nonprofit organizations and government agencies—all realized that they needed to build their own networks to operate successfully in the current environment. Brick-and-mortar operations, such as booksellers Barnes & Noble and Borders, established Web sites so that their online presence complemented their physical stores.

Nonprofit organizations like the Red Cross have office space, which is linked by networks to their Web sites. Both in person and online, volunteers can sign up, donors can make

An effective computer networking system made it possible for staff at the American Red Cross to get help to victims when Hurricane Katrina struck the Gulf Coast in 2005.

contributions, and people in need can turn to the organization for help. Even more important, organizations are able to keep people constantly updated on their latest projects, initiatives, and activities. For example, if the Red Cross needs to rally support for those in a flood-stricken area, as it did with Hurricane Katrina in 2005, it can channel supplies and money through its network to those in need while keeping people informed about how the fund-raising drive is going and how the response to the emergency is proceeding.

While workers for nonprofits may put in long hours at a disaster site, network engineers contribute to the effort by making sure that the organization's network is running problem-free during this critical time.

Networks enable legitimate small businesses to be home-based, rather than requiring them to rent office space. They allow an entire e-commerce shopping site like eBay to list, auction, and sell millions of items a day without having to store any of those items in one central location.

BOLSTERING THE BOTTOM LINE

Networks help businesses bolster their bottom line. Making a profit in business means finding ways to do things better and more economically. Networking enables a business to accomplish these goals. By sharing data, several people in one accounting department can simultaneously work on the same spreadsheet at their own workstations. Multiple salespeople can take orders from different people at the same time, increasing the speed with which orders are processed and shipped. Instead of buying printers for every computer, a number of computers can be networked to share one printer, which saves money on costly equipment. High-speed Internet connections and hard drives can also be shared, with networking again saving on service and equipment.

Besides enabling people to share information, networking allows for the sharing of resources. The person who makes this happen—and helps companies and organizations operate more cost-effectively and efficiently—is the network engineer.

NETWORK ENGINEERS: AT GROUND ZERO OF MODERN TECHNOLOGY

Network engineers are needed to set up computer networks everywhere, including in homes and schools, multinational corporations and military bases, and even small auto-repair shops and sprawling automobile-manufacturing plants. Network engineers are at the hub of the action when it comes to networking. While every company wants an efficient networking system, few people in most firms understand the inner workings of network hardware and software well enough to set up these systems themselves. That is where network engineers come in.

Some networks require so much attention that several network engineers work on them full time. Massive network operations, such as those spanning the country or several continents, may need to have a team of network engineers on the job twenty-four hours a day, seven days a week. For example, the United Nations, the U.S. Department of Justice, and the lumber and home-improvement store Lowe's all have large teams of network engineers attending to their intricate national and international computer networks.

While certain networks are complicated and wide-ranging, others have a relatively simple design. The bigger the operation, the more complicated the network, and the more people expect from the network. The increasing demands on the system keep the network engineer on the move. With the chance of a computer network glitch looming at any moment, a network engineer's job is rarely dull.

CONTEMPORARY NETWORKS

Networks are configured in various ways, depending on the needs of the users. All networks start out with a group of people who want to share information, a group of computers, and the connections between them. Variations are based on the amount of information being shared, the speed of the connections, the number of people with access to the network, whether the network is public or private, whether it is wireless or not, security considerations, and the kinds of computers being connected.

LOCAL AND METROPOLITAN AREA NETWORKS

Local area networks (LANs) are relatively small and are not run over public facilities. They can be in just one building or a suite of offices. Short-range technologies are the heart and soul of these networks. The company setting up the LAN generally has complete control over the network. A LAN makes it possible for only those in the organization to share information, and it offers no threat of an outside intruder.

KEEP INFORMED

Keeping informed of the latest news in network engineering is a good habit to adopt. That means staying on top of the latest technological innovations, as well as breaking news on the business side of network engineering.

For instance, when Hewlett-Packard announced that it had reached an agreement to purchase 3Com in November 2009, that announcement sent shock waves through the computer networking community, especially HP's leading competitor, Cisco. The merger meant that HP would gain entrée to China, one of the fastest-growing tech markets in the world. It also meant that those in the networking field would be watching to see how fast HP could integrate products from 3Com into its company and how easily HP would be able to offer the customer support for those products.

These types of events shape the work environment that surrounds network engineering. People who follow these stories gain important insights into where the field is heading and what the future holds for the information technology industry as a whole.

A network engineer may be asked to design a local area network that admits some outside users, such as suppliers or clients, as well. But most of the time, LANs are for internal company use only. Many schools and school districts use these kinds of networks.

Metropolitan area networks (MANs) connect computers in buildings that are located in a larger geographic area or spread across a campus. These networks are used to connect the computers of a company with many offices in a metropolitan area like New York City, but can even extend a bit farther afield. Many companies in New York City that use these networks also have offices in neighboring New Jersey and network to those offices by means of a MAN. Many LANs are interconnected by a metropolitan area network through the use of high-capacity technology, also known as backbone technology.

WIDE AREA NETWORKS

Because most networks provide access to a vast amount of information, most companies opt for a wide area network (WAN). These networks are usually run over publicly owned lines and are not owned by any one entity or group of entities. The Internet is a good example of a WAN; anyone can gain access to it. Every e-commerce business uses the Internet to open up its business to customers all over the world.

VIRTUAL PRIVATE NETWORKS

Virtual private networks (VPNs) can extend anywhere over public facilities, but privacy is guaranteed by encryption, or coding. Only the people the company wants to grant access to can get information through a VPN by means of a password.

When the information leaves one computer in the virtual private network, it is encrypted by means of a code and travels through a private pathway across the Internet to a recipient's computer, where the information is decoded. No one can read any of the information while it is being transmitted.

With more than 76 percent of Americans now using computers at home and at work, says a survey commissioned by Seagate Technology, network engineers are being called on to create and upgrade networks on a regular basis. Job opportunities in network engineering abound when it comes to working with giant networks. But much more limited networks, such as those in small businesses and homes, also need individual attention. There, too, network engineers can find high-paying jobs.

Because many people find the concept of networking intimidating, network engineers fill a crucial need. They are the professionals who turn a somewhat daunting task into a simple, workable system that everyday computer users can navigate with ease.

CHAPTER 2

What Is Network Engineering?

Network engineers hold a position of great responsibility: Now and in the foreseeable future, they are the people who are going to make or break the computer infrastructure of any organization. They are the ones who decide what type of network is needed and what type of hardware and software is required to make the network come together and function smoothly. Network engineers have to make many important decisions when setting up a network, including how much memory is needed for the system to operate properly. A bad decision regarding memory could spell disaster for a network.

Once the network is up and running, the network engineer's success is gauged by negatives: nothing disastrous is happening. Nobody notices that the system is working well; employees only notice when the system is not working. It is the job of the network engineer to make sure that the network is running so efficiently that, outside of the information technology department, nobody thinks much about it. Most people involved in businesses and organizations that use networks are not computer-savvy, and the last thing they want to hear is that the work they are doing is being hampered by computer network malfunctions. Network engineering is not a career for someone who needs constant attention and praise for excellent performance. Usually working quietly, behind the scenes, the network engineer realizes that a good day's work means that all the company employees were able to accomplish what they had to because the computer network operated flawlessly.

NETWORK ENGINEERING: THE BASICS

A network is made up of the information that needs to be shared (primarily files), computers (both hardware and software), and the connections between those computers. It is the job of the network engineer to create the network, maintain

At the AT&T Broadband Network Operations Center in Sacramento, systems engineer Bob MacMillan monitors the network that delivers broadband Internet service to millions of customers.

it, and keep it running smoothly and securely. The network model varies, based on the security needs of network users and the amount of information being exchanged. Also factored in are the number and types of computers being used, how many people will be communicating over the network, and, most recently, whether the network will be wireless or not.

DETERMINING THE NETWORK'S GOALS

The first job of the network engineer is fact finding—determining what the organization using the network needs and wants from it. Needs and wants can be two different things. Managers often have ambitious goals for the network, far beyond the organization's needs and financial means. As a result, the network engineer must find out what needs to be accomplished before creating the network. What are the goals of the network? What actually needs to be accomplished by the network? The best networks are the ones that accomplish the necessary goals at the lowest possible cost and have room to grow.

Good network engineers put together a network that serves the users and is easy to explain to them. To do this, the top network engineers study all the different operating systems and know how they work. Many companies today have a mix of systems in their laptops and desktop computers. Knowing how all the operating systems work is the best way to be prepared to set up a network in any company. Network engineers who work with only certain operating systems, say, just Microsoft or Novell, limit their job opportunities, taking themselves out of the running for jobs open to those who have a broad-based background in all sorts of operating systems.

PLANNING: A KEY STEP

Planning the network is one of the most important aspects of building any network. Many people are in such a hurry to set up a network that they rush through, or even overlook, the very important step of planning. Poor planning—that is, failing to think through all the possible alternatives—can slow down the whole operation. When a network plan is properly crafted, all the issues that face the project can be reviewed and checked before the network is put in place.

Proper planning allows the network engineer to make sure that all the components of the network will operate well together, necessary applications will work in the network, and the network will perform up to the required speed that is necessary. Careful checking and reviewing of the network plan helps prevent delays once work on building the network gets under way and keeps the organization from purchasing unnecessary equipment. Even when the planning stage is completed, the network can still be changed as it is being built, but proper planning will ensure that the network engineer does not have to make major changes, which often stall a project for long periods.

WRITING IT DOWN

When the network plan is completed, it is a good idea to write it down in detail in order to have a record of it. That way, the network engineer has a blueprint to refer to, rather than having to build the network from memory. Then, if a problem arises, the network engineer can review the plan and take

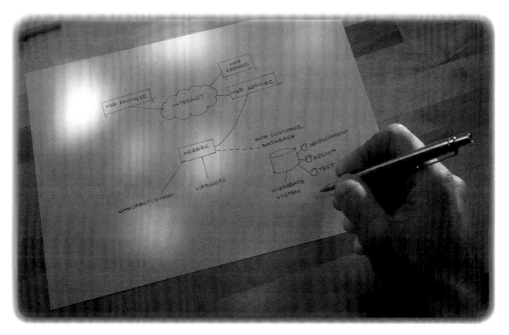

Diagramming a computer network is the first step a network engineer takes to design an effective, secure system. The diagram becomes a key reference tool when putting the actual network in place.

note of the reasoning behind various aspects of that plan. It is a lot easier to research the reason behind why certain things were done when there is a written record than to have to try to reconstruct the reasoning behind making a particular decision from scratch.

Keeping the written copy of the network plan updated is a good idea. If any changes are made in the network, those changes should be recorded. The written plan should be a handy reference tool that the network engineer can turn to when problems arise and simple questions need to be answered about how the network was designed, built, and revised. Keeping the written network plan in a loose-leaf binder allows the plan to be easily updated.

NETWORKING AMONG NETWORK ENGINEERS

Network engineers usually stay in touch with other network engineers and exchange ideas and information. Many even ask colleagues to review a network design plan to see if they spot any flaws or have an alternative way of building a particular aspect of the network. Having another set of eyes review a network plan confirms that everything that needs to be in the plan is included. Top network engineers always have people they can turn to for advice. Whether it is a former coworker, a teacher, or a classmate, even the experts sometimes need help in solving difficult computer networking problems.

CONFIGURING THE NETWORK

Starting with the basics, such as servers, switches, routers, and protocols, network engineers carefully configure a company's network.

SERVERS

For the most part, servers are the elite computers in the network: They have the most power and are the most expensive. Servers contain the resources that are going to be shared by all the other computers in the network, known as clients. Servers contain resources like e-mail, disk storage, and Internet access. The client computers are the ones that are used to access these resources.

ROUTERS AND SWITCHES

Routers and switches work together. The routers forward the information being sent or requested and determine the best route by which to send that information. The switches are the electronic or mechanical devices that control the flow of information through the circuits. The term "network topology" is used to explain how various components in the network are connected. The network engineer is the one who decides how that topology will take shape.

PROTOCOLS

The rules and regulations for getting and sending information through the network are called protocols. Many aspects of life are guided by protocols. For example, if someone would like to

NOTHING PERSONAL

The whole point of being a network engineer is to put networks together. But once a computer becomes part of a network, it loses its cachet as a "personal" computer. That is one of the points a network engineer has to communicate to network members. Once they are part of a network, computer users cannot just delete files anymore; someone else might need them. Network users may find that viruses can infect computers more easily, and security may be a much greater concern than it ever was before the network was installed.

People new to the network must recognize these issues. It is up to the network expert—that is, the network engineer—to point out all the advantages of the network and that those advantages outweigh the loss of personal independence that the non-network user once enjoyed.

get news about an event published in the school district newsletter, chances are there is a protocol, or a set of rules, that will have to be followed so that the information reaches the proper school officials, who need to get it approved for inclusion in the newsletter. The same is true with computer networks. In order for network communication to be effective, certain rules and regulations have to be followed by those using the network.

Today, there are standard network protocols, but that was not always the case. Each computer manufacturer used to have its own protocols for networking when computers first hit the market. That made it impossible to mix and match equipment from various manufacturers and combine it into one network. There are now industrywide, standard protocols that are not controlled by any one manufacturer. As long as these standards are followed, equipment from various manufacturers can coexist on one network. Network engineers must study these protocols and have a complete understanding of these standards.

Many organizations are involved in establishing standard protocols for computer networks. Those organizations include the Institute of Electrical and Electronics Engineers (IEEE), the World Wide Web Consortium (W3C), and the International Organization for Standardization (ISO). Network engineers must be aware of the latest protocols established for networking. This is crucial information when it comes to designing, building, and maintaining a network. Fortunately, the latest protocol information is readily available from the organizations mentioned above, as well as other organizations involved in networking that want to keep this vital information flowing to all who need it.

CHAPTER 3

How to Get Started: Education and Training

The most important trait that a person can bring to the field of network engineering is a love of computers. From there, training for a job as a network engineer follows naturally.

SPECIALTY COURSES IN HIGH SCHOOL

The first step is to take just about every course in computer science that is available at the high school level. Some high schools have more advanced computer science courses than others, but any high school courses in the subject will give students an idea as to whether or not working with computers is the right career choice for them. These classes will also give prospective network engineers an edge in their postsecondary education.

High school guidance counselors can be a good source of information when it comes to courses outside school. Guidance counselors know if any area corporations provide computer science classes for high school students. These courses might be offered either for high school credit or as extracurricular activities so that students can expand their knowledge of computer science, computer networks, and information technology in general.

Sometimes, corporations will present these classes to get young people interested in the IT field. Students attending these company-sponsored classes have an opportunity to

At the Farragut High School library in Chicago, student Valisha Powell installs a network interface card as part of a program to learn about wired and wireless networks.

meet people in the corporate world who work with computers on a daily basis and ask these experts work-related questions. They can also get to know people in the field who can give them advice on career paths, become mentors, or offer them entrée into the field itself.

Area colleges—both two-year and four-year institutions—may offer computer science programs specifically for high school students, or they may allow talented high school students to audit college courses in computer science. Generally speaking, college courses designed for high school students are intended to recruit more young people to fill the growing number of jobs in the information technology field.

Some high schools may not offer many computer science courses. But there is still a great deal of information about the field of network engineering available on the Internet and through a variety of books. Reviewing this information will give young people who are interested in setting up and maintaining computer networks a chance to see if network engineering is the field for them.

POSTSECONDARY EDUCATION

Once students graduate from high school, there are many routes for them to take to continue getting the education they need to become a network engineer. A college degree is still not necessary to find work as a network engineer, but employers are looking for people who have a solid foundation in computer science for network engineering positions. So learning as much as possible about the information technology field will always give applicants a leg up. As more colleges offer degrees in network engineering, employers will seek out applicants with a college background, making it tougher for those who have not gone the college route.

TECHNICAL SCHOOLS

The first places that most people look to get an education in network engineering are postsecondary technical schools. These schools offer first-rate classes in network engineering, as well as other information technology disciplines. It is worthwhile for high school sophomores or juniors to visit a few of these technical schools before submitting an application to get a good idea of what they offer and find out what is required for admission.

TWO-YEAR COLLEGES

Two-year colleges offer degrees in computer science and information technology. While technical schools may limit their network engineering curriculum to computer science courses, a two-year college might require students to take more introductory courses, such as English and math, along with computer science classes. A two-year college may afford students the opportunity to study more than one computer specialty, too. For instance, those who want to specialize in network engineering

Many high schools enable students to learn about the latest developments in information technology. At Wootton High School in Rockville, Maryland, student interns (from left) Sam Su, Darwin Mach, and Aaron Sampliner hone their IT skills.

may also be able to take courses in software development and database design at a two-year or community college, and that increases their value in the job market.

Again, it is worthwhile to visit some of these two-year colleges. Students can compare the programs and the admissions requirements of the colleges with those of the technical schools. They have to determine which type of institution offers them the type of education that best meets their goals. For instance, technical courses might be more advanced at a technical school than at a two-year college because a technical school's courses are primarily aimed at teaching the information required for the certifications that network engineers need to advance in their field (see chapter 4, "Getting Certified"). On the other hand, employers might consider a degree from a two-year college more prestigious than one from a technical school.

The key point to remember is that to join the ranks of working network engineers, newcomers to the field must have the skills to compete, so educational decisions need to be made based on where students can best acquire those skills. When visiting these schools, students should ask questions like the following:

- Where have the school's graduates found jobs? Talking to some of the graduates may help prospective students determine how well the school has met its graduates' needs.

- Does the school offer on-the-job training and help students find jobs? Dropping by the school's career services, or placement, office will give students a chance to see if internships and job fairs are posted.

- Does the school work with any area corporations so that students can observe network engineers on the job?

- Does the school teach the very latest technology? And, as technology changes, does the school offer courses to keep students up-to-date on the latest advancements?

- Can former students always turn to the school to update their skills?

FOUR-YEAR COLLEGES

Some people choose to go to a four-year college and take computer science courses that will help them enter the field of network engineering once they complete a four-year education. These people might even major in a field other than computer science while picking up the skills they need to become a network engineer. This approach gives students keen insights into other fields, such as finance, marketing, or business administration, while providing them with the computer skills necessary to make an impact on the technical side of the business.

INTERNSHIPS

Four-year colleges, especially bigger ones, usually have information technology offices right on campus. This gives students a chance to land an on-campus internship in the field and gain some valuable on-the-job experience.

COURSES TO CONSIDER

There are some courses in high school that students who are thinking of going into network engineering should consider taking, even though these courses may not seem as though they would apply to information technology.

Since information technology is so integral to contemporary business, having some understanding of the business world would help anyone going into the field of network engineering. Learning what is important to business-people helps those designing networks understand what big and small businesses expect from their networks.

Having a better-than-average ability to type will serve people in network engineering well, especially since they will be using a keyboard on such a regular basis. It is amazing how many people demand the fastest computer equipment and connections, only to be slowed down by poor typing skills. Being able to use a keyboard does not make someone a skilled typist. Typing courses are still offered in many high schools.

Even if there are no on-campus internships available, which would be unlikely, having an IT operation on campus lets students witness firsthand the type of work environment that they are thinking of entering.

Network engineering internships are valuable because on-the-job training, even if it is not paid training, always helps network engineers gain some insight into, as well as an in-depth understanding of, the business for which they are building a computer network. This gives them a better handle on what the business is trying to accomplish, what problems need to be solved by the network, and how the network eventually needs to grow and develop. With this type of understanding, network engineers can move from job to job within a field where they have a solid background.

For instance, a network engineer who began his or her career with an internship in a statewide bank and then was hired by that bank's network engineering department could easily move to a network engineering job in a nationwide or international banking operation. What is crucial to remember is that most of the advances that are being made in business today center around progress in the computer field. The latest innovations in banking, for example, do not revolve around banking per se (that is, lending, savings, and the like) as much as what the latest computer technology lets bank customers or employees do more easily, more quickly, more efficiently, and more securely. These computer advances are put in place by network engineers, whose success depends on developing these networks and keeping them operating problem-free.

ONLINE COURSES

Accredited courses and training programs in network engineering are available online. These courses of study usually take between eighteen months and two years to complete, and students must meet all the requirements of the program to be awarded a degree. Students can obtain two-year and four-year degrees in network engineering online and even go on to earn a master's degree in the subject. The University of

Southern California in Los Angeles; East Carolina University in Greenville, North Carolina; and the University of Illinois at Chicago are among the schools that offer online network engineering courses.

Studying online offers convenience, especially for working students. Students can arrange to take courses at any time in any place. Of course, this is all made possible by networks. Students who have studied at other schools, attending on-campus classes, may even be able to apply credit from the courses they took to these online programs.

Taking online courses is just like attending classes on a campus. Students have to make sure that the online program they choose is right for them. In addition, they must have the discipline required to complete the coursework outside the normal classroom environment.

Networks are complicated to maintain, so those going into the field of network engineering will have their knowledge of the inner workings of networks tested every day. As a result, they need as extensive an educational background in the field as they can get.

CHAPTER 4

Getting Certified

In the early days, many network engineers were self-taught. Eventually, their on-the-job experience and the expertise that they brought to handling computers helped them advance in their jobs. These people had almost no choice but to teach themselves the skills that they needed, since there were very few educational institutions that offered training in network engineering.

CERTIFICATION IS PARAMOUNT

Now things are different, with technical schools and both two-year and four-year colleges offering courses—if not degrees—in information technology and computer engineering. Though it is still possible to be self-taught and find a job in network engineering, many companies are looking for network engineers who, at the very least, hold some certifications in the field. Even people with college degrees are encouraged to get certifications to enhance their résumés.

These certifications go beyond the basic college degrees and act as proof that a network engineer has specific knowledge of vital software and hardware being used in the field. Various certifications, along with a degree, will help candidates looking for jobs in network engineering get higher-paying positions at better companies, advance through the ranks at whichever company they choose to join, and gain recognition in the network engineering field.

Several of the students in Jeff Ingram's computer class in Lebanon, Virginia, are Cisco certified and can work on routers that will eventually be used to construct a computer network.

VENDOR-SPECIFIC VS. VENDOR-NEUTRAL CERTIFICATIONS

Network engineering certifications are usually named after the company that manufactures the hardware or software that the network engineer is being credited with having mastered. Those types of certifications are known as vendor-specific. Companies like Microsoft, Cisco, Oracle, Novell, and Sun Microsystems (Java) award vendor-specific certifications. These companies offer all kinds of certifications, and new ones are being developed all the time. Many of these vendors have set up testing sites where the exams are given on a regular basis. Earning the designation as a Cisco Certified Network Associate (CCNA), for instance, indicates that the person with this certification has mastered the skills to install, troubleshoot, operate, and configure small to medium-sized networks using Cisco equipment.

The Computing Technology Industry Association (CompTIA), a nonprofit trade association, offers vendor-neutral certifications that are well respected in the field. Earning vendor-neutral certifications does not preclude network engineers from getting any vendor-specific certifications that they want as well.

THE VALUE OF EXPERIENCE

Prospective network engineers are usually advised to gain some experience in the networking field—whether it is in a volunteer capacity, an internship, or a part-time job—before taking any of the certification tests. CompTIA itself recommends that those considering taking its certification exams have at least nine months, or roughly five hundred hours, of work-related experience prior to taking the test.

Vendors also advise network engineers to spend some time working with the company's software and hardware before trying to get certified. Some companies will hire network engineers without certifications, especially if they have some on-the-job experience or a military background in computer networking, provided they agree to pursue certification within a specified period.

Gaining hands-on experience is the best way to prepare for the certification tests. Using the equipment, becoming familiar with the equipment, experimenting with the equipment, even working on equipment that is no longer in use in order to get a handle on diagnosing problems—all help network engineers prepare for the certification tests.

For example, prospective network engineers could practice configuring a network on computers at home. Practicing setting up networks over and over again is a good way to get familiar with the science underlying computer networks. Repetition is key to studying for the tests and gaining a mastery of the subject.

BOOT CAMPS

Some network engineers attend boot camps designed to give attendees days of intensive hands-on training in order to learn the skills needed to gain certification. Besides the hands-on training, boot camp attendees take practice tests to experience what the testing atmosphere is like and the format of the test.

There are plenty of practice tests that enable "campers" to determine which areas they need help with so that they can put special emphasis on studying those areas and practicing those aspects of the test. Practice tests also let candidates develop the proper test-taking mind-set, learn how to manage their time while taking the test, and read questions carefully to get a full understanding of them. The nonprofit CompTIA and schools like CED Solutions Computer Training Centers run fee-based camps.

ONLINE COURSES AND STUDY GUIDES

There are online courses that can help prospective test takers, as well as an array of study guides with CDs and training

Computer networks have opened up second careers for many people. John Sparenberg of Dallas, for instance, got his Microsoft certification after his position in another field was eliminated.

kits designed for people who prefer to work at their own pace as they study for the certification exams. This is in addition to "teach yourself" books that contain the entire coursework needed to learn how to become a network engineer. But nothing compares to the in-person classroom experience, where students have a chance to get instruction from a trained computer expert.

Network engineering is a technologically challenging field, and the certification exams in the field are challenging as well. But the tests also contain questions about issues that candidates will most likely face on the job at one time or another, such as troubleshooting and preventing data loss. These certifications are highly respected measures of proficiency in the IT field.

All the work put into passing the exams needed for certification is well worth the effort. Many network engineers find that they learn a great deal about the field just by preparing for the exams.

UPDATING CERTIFICATIONS

Some of the certifications require a single test; others require a series of tests. There is no limit to the number of certifications that network engineers can obtain. They are encouraged to update their certifications when the tests are revised to include questions about the latest technology. Usually, vendors will notify those who have passed their certification exams when those certifications should be updated. If network engineers are keeping abreast of and working with the latest innovations in the field, passing the latest version of the certification exam should not be difficult. Network engineers with the latest certifications show their employers that they are keeping up with all the advancements in the field and are familiar with the groundbreaking equipment literally flooding the market.

These certification exams were never designed to be once-in-a-lifetime tests. Because this technology is changing so rapidly, one of the biggest responsibilities of network engineers is to keep learning and stay current when it comes to the latest trends in the field. Hence, there is the need to pass the latest versions of these certification exams.

The exams test an applicant's full range of knowledge in using the equipment necessary in network engineering. Certification tests are not easy and are getting harder all the time, but a passing grade means that the successful candidate has a solid grasp of the field of network engineering. The types of questions are changing all the time but include multiple-choice questions with single answers, multiple-choice questions with multiple answers, true-false questions, fill-in-the-blanks, drag-and-drop, and router simulations. The tests are usually timed, lasting seventy-five to ninety minutes.

There is a fee for taking the certification tests, but those who fail can take the tests again. Failure should not discourage someone from taking an exam again. There are many reasons why people fail the tests, including just not being good at taking tests. Going through the testing experience one time helps some people get into the proper mind-set for taking the tests. Then they find they have an easier time the second time around, and they go on to pass other certification exams with much greater ease.

WHICH CERTIFICATIONS TO PURSUE

Knowing which certifications to get can be tricky, but working network engineers can always go for any additional certifications that they might need. The best way to determine which certifications to pursue is to research which vendors are being used heavily in a particular field. For instance, if most banking institutions are using a particular vendor for network equipment and a person is interested in pursuing a network engineering career in banking, that particular vendor's certifications would be the ones to go after.

Staying on top of the latest industry trends is another way to figure out which certifications are highly sought after. CompTIA recently determined that the hot-button certification now and for some time to come is security, with two-thirds of information technology workers intending to get some type of certification in a security discipline within the next five years. As more and more business is conducted over networks, the concern over security keeps growing. Network engineers want to be able to address those concerns by having the ability to provide the best possible security for the most complicated networks. One of the fastest-growing security certifications is in the field of computer forensics, the branch of investigation that involves discovering, processing, and using legal evidence gathered from computers.

According to CompTIA, putting together an impressive portfolio of certifications has two main goals: personal growth and economic advancement. Some of the certifications show that network engineers are ready for advancement, such as going from one level of network engineering to a higher level. Others demonstrate a grasp of new knowledge. For instance, a certified network engineer might add certifications in other aspects of his or her field, such as green information technology and security.

SOME SAMPLE QUESTIONS

Here are some sample questions from the Microsoft Certified Systems Engineering (MCSE) certification exam. Questions from other vendors' exams are similar to these:

1. Windows 2000 Professional is able to access drives compressed with DriveSpace.

    A. True
    B. False

2. What is another name for 10BaseT?

    A. Baseband
    B. Broadband
    C. Thicknet
    D. Thinnet
    E. Twisted Pair

3. Which component of the Windows 2000 Executive is responsible for handling input and output from installed devices?

    A. The Device Manager
    B. The Cache Manager
    C. The I/O Manager
    D. None of the above

4. Before upgrading to Windows 2000, you should turn off or uninstall virus-protection software.

    A. True
    B. False

5. If a network has a Windows NT domain controller, what kind of network is it?

    A. WAN
    B. High-speed
    C. Peer-to-peer
    D. Server-based
    E. Server-to-server

ANSWERS

1. B. False

2. E. Twisted Pair

3. C. The I/O Manager

4. A. True

5. D. Server-based

CHAPTER 5

On the Job

Network engineering is a job that requires stamina, quick reactions, and alertness. Long hours are often involved because most organizations would like to have any maintenance that needs to be done on their computer networks performed during off-hours to avoid any disruptions during normal working hours. That leaves evenings, overnight, and weekends, and those hours are in addition to a normal shift because network engineers have to be on the job during regular business hours to make sure that the network is running smoothly then as well. Big businesses and organizations have a team of network engineers to share the workload, but smaller operations may have just one person to handle the entire network operation.

There are many aspects to a network engineer's job besides making sure that the internal network is up and running without a hitch. Network engineers have to monitor the network, constantly being on the lookout for ways to make the network run better. It is the job of the network engineer to catch problems before they happen. Monitoring how employees use the Internet and the network is essential. Also, making recommendations for improving and upgrading the network before employees start complaining about how the network is operating keeps a network engineer ahead of the curve. Cost-efficient improvements, upgrades, and updates should always be a top priority. This shows that

Network engineering is so popular that people have camps to exchange ideas about the latest technology. These networking enthusiasts gather at a former Soviet airbase in Finowfurt, Germany.

those working in the information technology department share a concern for the business's bottom line.

Network engineers should always stay on top of the latest hot-button issues in the industry, such as going green. In recent years, there has been a major focus on making sure that networks are as energy-efficient as possible. Knowing how to build and maintain a network that is environmentally friendly, yet economical, falls back on network engineers, who have to be able to explain to those in charge why networks were set up the way they were.

SECURITY CONCERNS

Managing viral protection and monitoring antispam strategies are high on a network engineer's to-do list, since network security is one of the leading aspects of the job. Security is a major concern today: no matter how trustworthy employees may seem and how friendly an office environment is, network engineers must be concerned about both internal and external security.

First of all, security breaches can happen accidentally. Not every employee is a computer expert; in fact, most are not. Someone can gain access to confidential information with a careless click of a mouse or by calling up the wrong file. The network has to safeguard against these types of mishaps.

A disgruntled employee can damage network files if proper security measures are not in place. Though there may appear to be no unhappy employees on the horizon, it cannot be taken for granted that there never will be. Good security can prevent this type of loss.

Outside forces like hackers always pose a risk, threatening to break into a network and steal personal information about employees and financial information about clients. This can lead to identity theft. Some hackers may not be interested in stealing information. Instead, they might just want to plant a virus and use the network they broke into to spread it.

Most networks connected to the Internet use firewalls as their first line of defense. A firewall prevents unauthorized access to a network or computer system and is usually part of any network design. Network engineers must stay alert on a daily basis to catch a security breach as soon as it happens, track down the source of the breach, and correct the problem. The better the security system that the network engineer has in place, the better the chance of limiting these breaches and keeping information secure.

Remember: If a network is connected to the Internet, those connections not only let users go outside the network, but they also let others—including hackers—come in. Hackers are constantly trying to pierce the armor of any security system, and new viruses are always being invented to infect networks and computers. That is why it is so important for network engineers to be vigilant; those who catch security breaches early are immensely valuable to their employers.

TROUBLESHOOTING

After setting up the network and making sure that it is as secure as possible, the next most important task for a network engineer is troubleshooting. Networks involve complicated configurations; they are made up of a lot of different parts. The bigger the network, the more parts there are, and the more that can go wrong.

Networks will break down. Solving the problem, or trouble-shooting, is a crucial part of the job of a network engineer. If an entire network goes down, business can be stalled for however long it takes to restore service. A few hours of no service can seem like an eternity when frantic workers are demanding to get the network back up and running.

Naturally, troubleshooting the network is easier if the same network engineer who built the network is working to repair it. But because that is not always the case, network engineers have to have a good handle on problem solving for every network that they oversee, regardless of whether they designed it or not.

KEEPING A CHECKLIST

Network engineers should know the network they are working with well enough to have a checklist that they can run down to see if they can diagnose a network failure quickly. They should have some type of action plan in place so that network breakdowns can be tackled in an organized fashion. There are many things that can go wrong in a computer network, and each problem has to be addressed in a methodical way. Duplication of effort only wastes time, so it is helpful to keep a record of what has been checked and what still needs to be examined.

Most network engineers will start their investigation with the obvious, such as making sure that everything is connected, and work toward the more obscure possible causes of a network breakdown. Sometimes, it helps to talk with the employee who first noticed the problem. That employee might have unknowingly done something that led to the failure. Finding the problem is like being a detective. Once the mystery is solved, network engineers usually write a report about the problem and how it was solved and put the report in the binder with the network plan (see chapter 2, "What Is Network Engineering?") so that they have something to refer to when another problem arises.

DISASTER PLANNING

What makes network engineering such an interesting occupation are the varied responsibilities that come with the job. Among those responsibilities is planning for a disaster—everything from vandalism and sabotage to floods and fires. Network engineers must have a plan in place for backing up

Computer networks have proved invaluable in tracking developing weather patterns. Eric Blake (in foreground), a specialist at the National Hurricane Center in Miami, tracks Hurricane Bill as it approaches the Atlantic coastline in 2009.

network data in the event of such a disaster. This usually adds some hours to the network engineer's job because the best time to run a backup program is during off-hours to make sure that everything being copied is up-to-date. If a backup program is running when employees are accessing files, there is always a chance that the backup program may skip over files that employees are working on while the backup program is operating. Having a way to back up data is essential. So is having a way to recover that data in the event of a disaster, small or large. Network engineers are the ones who are expected to develop and put in place this recovery plan.

Basically, a disaster plan—or a business continuity plan, as it is more commonly referred to in the boardroom—is a plan for how operations will continue in the event of a disaster. These plans have to take into account anything that might happen that would impact operations for any span of time. If a street collapse forces the headquarters of a business to close for a week, a good disaster plan will incorporate a way for employees to still access necessary business files and keep the operation going until the office can be reopened. Because so much is riding on keeping the computers running, the person who is going to keep the operation humming during times of disaster is the network engineer. The role can be likened to that of people in the local community years ago who were in charge of civil defense. Like civil defense officers, network engineers will get the call when disaster strikes, and their disaster plan will be put to the test.

Many network engineers prefer not to wait for disaster to strike to see if their plans to save the day will work. As a result, they will often schedule drills to see how effective their recovery and disaster plans are. If need be, they tweak the plans

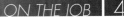

AND NOW FOR A WORD . . .

People interested in a career as a network engineer might not consider taking a course in public speaking. Yet network engineers spend a great deal of time speaking to the public—or, at least, employees in their companies. Once a network is put in place, the network engineer is usually asked to explain the network to those who are using it. This is a challenge because the computer expert has to explain this technical subject in layman's terms so that even a person who knows very little about computers can understand it.

It is not the job of the network engineer to confuse the audience or bore them, but to get them excited about this technological new world that they are entering, answer their questions clearly, and allay their fears. That is why it is not a bad idea for network engineers to take a course in public speaking. That way, they are comfortable talking in front of people and presenting the topic they are talking about in a fun, interesting, and intriguing way.

and do another drill. Some will do drills on a fairly regular basis to make sure that their plans are ready to implement at a moment's notice.

Disasters vary for different companies. A prolonged power failure may be disastrous for a telemarketing firm but manageable for a rug cleaning service that does most of its business off premises. The network engineer for the telemarketing company would need to create a disaster plan that would keep the company operating in the event of such a power failure. But that is all in a day's work for a network engineer.

When it comes to network engineering, the jobs are everywhere. But it is worthwhile for prospective network engineers to do the research necessary to learn exactly where the best jobs are and where the jobs that they would find most challenging and fulfilling are. Some fields, such as banking, have been involved with networking for a long time, and that gives network engineers a chance to become part of an industry where network expertise has been relied on for years. Other fields, such as health care, have not used networking to its fullest potential, so network engineers pursuing jobs in that field can get a toehold in an area where networking will be growing at an ever-increasing pace for some time to come.

HEALTH CARE: A GROWTH FIELD

While openings for network engineers are plentiful in law enforcement, education, government, finance, and business in general, experts agree that the biggest growth area is health care. Because digitizing health records is a high priority when it comes to improving health care, there should be massive job openings for network engineers in hospitals and other health care facilities for the foreseeable future. But health care has other needs as well. Health care agencies have put their money into medical equipment, not computer network

The next frontier for network engineering is medical records. This disk, containing medical information parents have inputted about their children, can be given to camps, schools, or daycare centers in case of a medical emergency.

infrastructure. So when it comes to networking technology, the health care industry needs some resuscitation.

Networks in hospitals especially need to be updated, since so much more can now be accomplished by using these networks than could be when they were first set up. Cisco, for example, has a technology called HealthPresence that allows a doctor to examine a patient, even though the doctor is not physically present at the hospital. A nurse or other health care practitioner connects medical instrumentation to the patient, and the doctor can then conduct the examination and interact with the patient.

Computer networks in hospitals have to be precise and efficient. Only top performance will do. Doctors will be put off by a slow network. So the network is going to have to perform well every time, or physicians simply will not use it. Such a setting would be ideal for network engineers looking for a fast-paced work environment that operates twenty-four hours a day, seven days a week with little room for error.

As computer networking grows in the health care industry, related fields like medical insurance will have to keep up with it. While insurers have been using networking for some time, the use of electronic record keeping in health care will spur network updating in the insurance field, too.

DOING THE RESEARCH

Another growth area is e-commerce, as business over the Internet continues to grow and companies continue to strive to offer more products and faster service. Financial institutions are adding new services to make doing online transactions not only more convenient but also more secure. Local small businesses are trying to keep up with bigger competitors by offering more online options, and network engineers are needed to build and maintain those smaller networks.

The old-fashioned way of job hunting—pounding the pavement—is no longer the norm. But doing the proper research to evaluate the employment picture in a particular area still is. It helps to become familiar with the business landscape; that is, determining which types of businesses predominate in a particular area. There are so many jobs available for qualified network engineers that a simple call to an organization's IT department will most likely reveal that there are openings there for network engineers. Try not to wait until the last minute to start searching the marketplace for leads on job openings. Do research several years before entering the job market to try to pinpoint areas where network engineers are needed.

Several Web sites contain news about industries that are looking to expand network systems. Undoubtedly, some have offices nearby. Check the want ads in your area to see which industries are looking for network engineers and what the requirements are for those positions, including desired certifications and experience.

GAINING EXPERIENCE

While there are tests to get certified, getting experience could be a bit tougher. Experience is the most important element on a candidate's résumé for any position. Yet here is the puzzler: Employers always want to know the professional background of people they are thinking about hiring, and young people going into the business world want to know how they can get experience if nobody will hire an inexperienced person.

VOLUNTEERING

One answer is to volunteer. The only way that many nonprofit organizations can get computers is by having them donated. But once those computers are donated, the organizations have to rely on the know-how of either their own employees or volunteers to keep those computers operating efficiently.

One of the services desperately needed by such nonprofits is network engineering. A trained network engineer can get lots of experience working on the computers of either large or small nonprofit organizations. Volunteer network engineers will come across all the real-world problems they will face on the job and be able to devise timely, practical solutions that can help build a strong résumé—and a strong community. Volunteers should make note of the network problems that they came across in their volunteer work and show potential employers (on their résumé or during an interview) what creative ideas they used to solve those problems. There may even be opportunities to provide these services to more than one worthy community organization. In addition, there are often internships available to network engineers trying to amass some on-the-job experience.

Choosing the right field in which to do volunteer work or an internship is as important as choosing the right job. For instance, those who would like to go into computer networking in the medical field should look toward doing their volunteer work at a community clinic or a nonprofit hospital. This gives prospective network engineers the chance to see if they enjoy working in the medical field. They also get a sense of what type of networking work needs to be done in that area and which certifications to pursue.

Network engineers play an important role in various industries. Loie Gaillac, lead engineer for Edison International in Pomona, California, uses a network to monitor a battery test for an electric car.

JOB REQUIREMENT: IMPECCABLE ETHICAL CHARACTER

Network engineers are guardians of very sensitive information. They have access to a company's most private records, as well as employee and customer information that simply cannot be exposed to outsiders. Part of the job makes network engineers responsible for passwords and control of who has access to the network and the network's data. This trust can never be violated, and an organization's security can never be compromised.

It is understandable that a company looking for a network engineer would want to make sure that the person being hired for this sensitive position is absolutely trustworthy. No candidates for a network engineering position would be hired if they had a criminal record, even for something that might seem to be a minor transgression. Besides having a solid grasp of the technology underlying network engineering, prospective network engineers must be honest, trustworthy, and ethically beyond reproach.

FULFILLING TWO GOALS AT ONCE

In some cases, network engineering offers people a rare opportunity to fulfill dual career goals. First, it enables people who love computers and want to be on the cusp of the latest technological innovations to take that technology as far as it will go. Second, it allows them to apply their technical knowledge to another field that they have always had a passion for and wanted to work in, such as law enforcement or international banking. For instance, someone with an interest in telecommunications can seek networking jobs in the telecommunications field. Those enthusiastic about education can use network technology to help colleges expand their educational offerings not only in the local community but also throughout the region or even around the world. Networking could help a disabled person get an education without having to commute to school, for example. Someone drawn to health care could pursue networking jobs in that field and help make meaningful contributions to the advancement of medical science.

Like having a dual major in college, where students pursue two fields of study intensively, network engineers can use their technological expertise to spur progress in another profession that they also find compelling. Almost any field that a person has an interest in can benefit from the latest network technology.

Having a background in banking can lead a network engineer on the path to making new inroads in the banking industry. Understanding the sporting goods business will help a network engineer find a way to use a network to get sporting goods designed in California to exercise enthusiasts all over the world. Someone committed to saving the environment can help spread the latest information about reducing people's carbon footprint to environmentalists all over the world. Having a good understanding of a field other than network engineering will allow network professionals to truly understand what is needed to advance these fields and make a contribution beyond their technical skills.

Once up-and-coming network engineers decide which field to specialize in, it is time to see what jobs are available. If a network engineer would like to work in government, he or she should find out which branches of government have openings. For law enforcement, the Federal Bureau of Investigation, the U.S. Postal Inspector Service, or the Secret Service might be good places to seek jobs. Those looking for government work dealing with the environment might want to explore the U.S. Environmental Protection Agency or a state environmental protection agency. Network engineers who are passionate about health care might consider applying to hospitals, pharmaceutical companies, or large drugstore chains.

CHAPTER 7

Turning Pro

While thirty-thousand-plus students go through their daily routine at George Mason University in Fairfax, Virginia, a hardworking team of highly trained computer specialists is making sure that the university's computer network system is up and running without a hitch. The university has a large network, with thirty-six thousand ports and a staff of thirty people, including twenty-four network engineers who work in the school's network engineering and technology department. Members of the department work long hours and are on call twenty-four hours a day, seven days a week. Located just minutes from the nation's capital, Washington, D.C., the university itself has done groundbreaking research in information technology, besides offering degrees in the subject and many other disciplines, including engineering, health care, and biotechnology.

With the luxury of a large staff, the university has different people to work on different aspects of the network, says Randy Anderson, director of the university's network engineering and technology department. At a small operation, one person might have to be a jack-of-all-trades, doing all the design work and maintenance on the network. But that network would be much smaller than George Mason University's. "The term 'network engineer' carries a broad range of duties, from the technician level to people who do very detailed design work that requires a master's degree," says Anderson.

Network engineers at George Mason University were instrumental in designing the computer system at the school's new data center in Fairfax, Virginia. Here, network engineering chief Randy Anderson inspects the wiring during the project.

DIVISION OF LABOR

Anderson describes the type of work his department is involved in on a day-to-day basis: "We have a staff of five advanced network engineers, senior-level people, who do the overall planning and design. The design encompasses a certain number of things because the underlying infrastructure has to be there. You have to have the cables in the right places and the right types of cables—fiber, Cat-6 cabling, and such—so we have a group of people who specialize in cabling matters, who just deal with the infrastructure side of things, making sure the duct banks between buildings go in the right direction, the manholes are in the right places, and so on. Then we have a group of people who work on optical networking. We have another team working on the more generic kind of things, such as deciding the types of routers we need in what locations and configuring the routers. All that requires extensive experience and training. Cisco certification helps out with that." In addition to this work, Anderson has a maintenance team that "is always busy because maintenance encompasses problem solving and troubleshooting in addition to the routine software updates."

Network engineers working on big systems like the one at George Mason University will find it helpful to have a telecommunications background in addition to a data background. "These days, network engineers are almost certainly going to be asked to work with the telephone systems to some extent because it is getting more and more common to have a converged voice and data network," says Anderson. Network engineers work with video aspects of networks as well.

With such a large system, there is always a chance that a user might inadvertently cause a problem in the network. It is up to the network engineers working in the maintenance department to track down the problem and correct it. As an example, Anderson points to the common user error of buying a wireless router in a local store and then plugging it in incorrectly; this disrupts the network. The maintenance team has to pinpoint the trouble quickly, find the user who caused the problem, and correct the situation before too many other users are affected by it.

Most people will get their start in network engineering in the maintenance group of a big operation like the one at George Mason University, according to Anderson: "Somebody who comes in with a two-year degree will go to our maintenance group, where they can start off by learning about our network, learn the basics of troubleshooting—working with routers and switches, and learning how to deal with the customers [users]. You have to demonstrate good customer service—that is really a must. So you have to master all those skills. If a person shows that they are really good at digging into the technical details, they may then be able to move up into the detailed design work."

George Mason University looks to hire network engineers who have certifications in products that are used in the university's network system. Other businesses and organizations seeking network engineers take the same approach. Anderson points out that if a network engineer is applying for a job at a particular company and knows that the company uses Cisco and Juniper products in its network, having certifications from those vendors would certainly help the applicant get seriously considered for the position.

But he also cautions not to overlook the importance of work experience: "For most of our positions, we want someone with work experience, and most places are like that. The best way to get that experience is to find an internship. If you can do that, it is fantastic experience. Five of the people working here started out as interns. Internships are far and away the best way of getting a foot in the door and proving that you have a real interest in network engineering."

INTERNSHIPS

Internships are extremely popular in the tech industry, as they are in many businesses today. Bringing interns onboard is an inexpensive way for companies to add a needed employee, and it gives young people a chance to gain experience at big companies that they may not have a chance of getting into otherwise. It also gives fledgling network engineers an opportunity to "try on" a profession, to see if the career choice they made is right for them.

Internships enable young people to put theories they learned in the classroom to the test in the real world. Most of these internships are nonpaying or low-paying positions, but they do count as on-the-job experience and sometimes lead to part-time or full-time jobs. The recommendations acquired by successfully completing these internships help in landing a job in the future, as do the contacts made during these internships.

THE INTERNSHIP INTERVIEW

Interviewing for an internship is much the same as interviewing for a job, but perhaps a bit more rigorous because so

Internships provide excellent training for prospective network engineers. Intern Maja Lakicevic learns about some new software while on the job at Menlo Innovations in Ann Arbor, Michigan.

many untested people are trying to break into a field like network engineering and believe that a particular internship is the way to do it. To stand out, an applicant should try to learn as much as possible about the company, organization, or government agency offering the internship. While it is important to have a strong network engineering background, applicants should be able to show that they know something about the product or service that the organization offers. Applicants who take the time to learn about the organization where they would like to get an internship show that they have initiative, as well as an interest, in what the employer does and how they can fit into that work environment.

TRAINING IN THE MILITARY

One of the best ways to learn technical skills like network engineering is in the military. Many network engineers train for their jobs by serving in the military, where they not only learn all the theory behind the technical skills they are being taught but also get actual hands-on experience in real-world situations. These trainees are paid while learning their skills. They then serve in many different capacities once they complete their training and are assigned a job in the armed forces.

The military's technical training has always been singled out for its excellence. In addition, the armed forces are noted for using the latest technology. So network engineers in every branch of the military get a chance to train and work with state-of-the-art equipment that has not yet made its way into civilian life. When they leave the military, many network engineers get jobs in the private sector using the experience that they gained in the armed services.

Because the network engineer's job is to help organizations advance technologically, knowing about a firm or organization gives applicants for internships valuable background knowledge so that they can ask insightful questions and give thoughtful answers during the internship interview. Showing an awareness of the company or organization's culture will always give applicants a leg up in getting hired, either as an intern or an employee.

KEEPING TRACK OF EXPERIENCE

Once young people have secured an internship, it is a good idea to take note of the various tasks that they performed while serving as an intern. This way, interns can give prospective employers a fairly detailed account of the on-the-job experience they gained. For example, if a problem came up on a network during the internship, make note of what was done to repair the network and what role you played in that repair. That would be an interesting subject to discuss in a future job interview. Just observing how the repair is done puts interns in the middle of the action and allows them to see network engineers working on actual network problems. That shows the kind of real-life work experience that the young person gained during the internship.

backbone A cable used to interconnect parts of a network to complete the path for information exchange.

backup A copy of data saved by either a different means or in a different place as a security measure.

computer forensics A division of computer science that deals with information and legal evidence gathered from computers; also known as digital forensics.

continuity An uninterrupted flow.

e-commerce Business conducted online.

encryption The coding of files so that they cannot be read by unauthorized personnel.

firewall A device that prevents unauthorized access to a network or computer.

Internet A globally interconnected computer network.

layman's terms Everyday language.

local area network (LAN) Small networks that are not run over public facilities.

network topology The way various components in the network are connected to each other.

optical networking The use of light to set up a communications network between computers, telephones, and other electronics.

protocol A set of rules and regulations for getting and sending information through the network.

router An electronic device used to forward information being sent or requested and determine the best route by which to send that information.

server The computer containing the resources that are going to be shared by all other computers in a network.

switch An electronic or mechanical device that controls the flow of information through the circuits.

vendor-neutral certification A certification offered by a nonprofit organization not affiliated with a particular company.

vendor-specific certification A certification named after the company that manufactures the hardware or software that the network engineer is being credited with having mastered.

wide area network (WAN) A large network that covers a wide geographic area and is run over publicly owned lines.

American Society for Engineering Education
(ASEE)
1818 N Street NW, Suite 600
Washington, DC 20036-2479
(202) 331-3500
Web site: http://www.asee.org
The ASEE is a nationwide society promoting excellence in
all areas of engineering and engineering technology
education.

American Society for Information Science & Technology
(ASIS&T)
1320 Fenwick Lane - Suite 510
Silver Spring, MD 20910
(301) 495-0900
Web site: http://www.asis.org
This professional organization is dedicated to the advance-
ment of information technology.

Association of Information Technology Professionals (AITP)
401 North Michigan Avenue, Suite 2400
Chicago, IL 60611-4267
(312) 245-1070
Web site: http://www.aitp.org
The AITP is a worldwide professional organization representing the interests and concerns of those employed in
the information technology industry.

Canadian Information Processing Society (CIPS)
5090 Explorer Drive, Suite 801
Mississauga, ON L4W 4T9
Canada
(877) 275-2477
Web site: http://www.cips.ca
The CIPS is a professional organization representing the
interests of information technology specialists in Canada.

Institute of Electrical and Electronics Engineers, Inc. (IEEE)
3 Park Avenue, 17th Floor
New York, NY 10016-5997
(212) 419-7900
Web site: http://www.ieee.org
The IEEE is recognized around the world as the leading
voice for engineering, computing, and technology information. Under its umbrella are a number of councils and
societies dealing with specific interests, such as the IEEE
the Computer Society.

The Internet Society (ISOC)
1775 Wiehle Avenue, Suite 201
Reston, VA 20190-5108
(703) 439-2120
Web site: http://www.isoc.org
This is a worldwide nonprofit organization created to
address issues relating to the future of the Internet, such
as Internet infrastructure standards.

Optical Society of America (OSA)
2010 Massachusetts Avenue NW

Washington, DC 20036
(202) 223-8130
Web site: http://www.osa.org
The OSA is an organization dedicated to the science and
   technology of light.

Society for Canadian Women in Science and Technology
471-411 Dunsmuir Street
Vancouver, BC V6B 1X4
Canada
(604) 893-8657
Web site: http://www.scwist.ca
This Canadian organization is dedicated to encouraging and
   helping women to enter the fields of science, engineering, and technology.

WEB SITES

Due to the changing nature of Internet links, Rosen
Publishing has developed an online list of Web sites related
to the subject of this book. This site is updated regularly.
Please use this link to access the list:

http://www.rosenlinks.com/cict/cine

For Further Reading

Alexander, Philip. *Home and Small Business Guide to Protecting Your Computer Network, Electronic Assets, and Privacy.* Westport, CT: Praeger, 2009.

Anderson, Al, and Ryan Benedetti. *Head First Networking.* Sebastopol, CA: O'Reilly, 2009.

Black, Uyless. *Sams Teach Yourself Networking in 24 Hours.* 4th ed. Indianapolis, IN: Sams, 2009.

Clarke, Glen E. *Mike Meyers' Certification Passport: CompTIA Network+.* 3rd ed. New York, NY: McGraw-Hill, 2009.

Derfler, Frank, Jr., and Les Freed. *How Networks Work.* 7th ed. Indianapolis, IN: Que, 2005.

Doherty, Jim, Neil Anderson, and Paul Della Maggiora. *Cisco Networking Simplified.* 2nd ed. Indianapolis, IN: Cisco Press, 2008.

Donahue, Gary. *Network Warrior.* Sebastopol, CA: O'Reilly Media, Inc., 2007.

Eberts, Marjorie, and Margaret Gisler. *Careers for Computer Buffs and Other Technological Types.* 3rd ed. New York, NY: McGraw-Hill, 2006.

Field, Shelly. *Career Coach: Managing Your Career in the Computer Industry.* New York, NY: Checkmark Books, 2009.

Gast, Matthew S. *802.11 Wireless Networks: The Definitive Guide.* 2nd ed. Sebastopol, CA: O'Reilly, 2007.

Gregson, Susan. *Cyber Literacy: Evaluating the Reliability of Data.* New York, NY: Rosen Publishing Group, 2008.

Hallberg, Bruce A. *Networking: A Beginner's Guide.* 5th ed. New York, NY: McGraw-Hill, 2010.

Henderson, Henry. *Career Opportunities in Computers and Cyberspace*. 2nd ed. New York, NY: Facts on File, 2004.

Information Technology Jobs in America: Corporate & Government Career Guide. New York, NY: Info Tech Employment, 2009.

Kirk, Amanda. *Field Guides to Finding a New Career: Information Technology*. New York, NY: Checkmark Books, 2009.

Kurose, James F., and Keith N. Ross. *Computer Networking: A Top-Down Approach Featuring the Internet*. Reading, MA: Addison-Wesley, 2007.

Lammle, Todd. *Cisco Certified Network Association Study Guide*. 6th ed. Hoboken, NJ: Wiley Publishing, 2007.

Meyers, Mike. *CompTIA Network+ Exam Guide*. 4th ed. New York, NY: McGraw-Hill, 2009.

Reeves, Diane Lindsey, Gail Korlitz, and Don Rauf. *Career Ideas for Teens in Information Technology*. New York, NY: Checkmark Books, 2006.

Schneier, Bruce. *Schneier on Security*. Hoboken, NJ: Wiley Publishing, 2008.

Walberg, Sean, Loyd Case, Joel Durham Jr., and Derek Torres. *Wireless All-in-One for Dummies*. 2nd ed. Hoboken, NJ: Wiley Publishing, 2010.

Bibliography

Anonopoulos, Andreas. "Green Enterprise: Three Networking Investments That Make a Difference." TechTarget, October 10, 2009. Retrieved December 1, 2009 (http://search networking.techtarget.com/tip/0,289483,sid7_gci1 371020_mem1,00.html?track=NL-81&ad=737957&Offer= mn_eh120109NETWUNSC&asrc=EM_USC_10148182& uid=9401860).

Berry, Charles W., and William H. Hawn Jr. *Computer & Internet Dictionary for Ages 9–99*. Hauppauge, NY: Barron's, 2000.

Burns, Julie Kling. *Opportunities in Computer Careers*. New York, NY: McGraw-Hill, 2002.

Carr, Nicholas G. *Does It Matter? Information Technology and the Corrosion of Competitive Advantage*. Boston, MA: Harvard Business Press, 2004.

Dubie, Denise. "Security Pros Seek Hacking, Forensics Skills." *Network World*, November 9, 2009. Retrieved November 15, 2009 (http://www.networkworld.com/ news/2009/110909-security-skills.html).

Gilster, Ron. *Cisco Networking for Dummies*. Hoboken, NJ: Wiley Publishing, 2002.

Hillstrom, Kevin. *Defining Moments: The Internet Revolution*. Detroit, MI: Omnigraphics, Inc., 2005.

Kearns, Dave. "Effective Identity Management Begins with Your Employees." *Network World*, December 3, 2008. Retrieved December 9, 2009 (http://www.networkworld. com/newsletters/dir/2008/120108id2.html).

Lancaster, Tom. "Network Engineering Overview:
    Techniques for Making Changes." TechTarget,
    August 21, 2006. Retrieved November 16, 2009 (http://
    searchnetworking.techtarget.com/tip/0,289483,sid7_
    gci1211274,00.html).

Lewis, Bob. *Keep the Joint Running: A Manifesto for 21st Century
    Information Technology.* Eden Prairie, MN: Survivor
    Publishing, 2009.

Lewis, Bob. *Learning IT: The Toughest Job in the World.* Eden
    Prairie, MN: Survivor Publishing, 2004.

Litchko, James P., Ron Lander, and Lew Wagner. *Cyber Threat
    Levels Response Handbook.* Rockville, MD: Know Book
    Publishing, 2004.

Litchko, James P., and Al Payne. *Know Cyber Risk: By
    Managing Your IT Security.* Rockville, MD: Know Book
    Publishing, 2004.

McGillicuddy, Shamus. "New Skills Emerge for
    Network Engineering and Administration Careers."
    TechTarget, June 18, 2009. Retrieved November 7,
    2009 (http://searchnetworking.techtarget.com/news/
    article/0,289142,sid7_gci1359629,00.html).

Morris, Michael. "More Thoughts on Network Engineers
    and the CCDE." *Network World,* November 5, 2007.
    Retrieved January 11, 2010 (http://www.networkworld.
    com/community/node/21969).

Oltsik, Jon. "Networking Nuggets and Security Snippets."
    Network World, January 8, 2010. Retrieved January 11,
    2010 (www.networkworld.com/community/node/
    50819).

Plotnick, Neil. "Testing and Planning for New Products."
    TechTarget, November 20, 2005. Retrieved November 16,

2009 (http://searchnetworking.techtarget.com/
loginMembersOnly/1,289498,sid7_gci782701,00.
html?NextURL=http%3A//searchnetworking.
techtarget.com/tip/0%2C289483%2Csid7_gci782701_
tax305162%2C00.html&app_code=90&).

Ross, John. *Network Know-How*. San Francisco, CA: No
Scratch Press, 2009.

Scarpati, Jessica. "Network Security Risks Multiply
When Enterprises Begin Outsourcing." TechTarget,
October 7, 2009. Retrieved December 1, 2009.
(http://searchnetworking.techtarget.com/news/
article/0,289142,sid7_gci1370642,00.html)

Viega, John. *The Myths of Security: What the Computer Security
Industry Doesn't Want You to Know*. Sebastopol, CA:
O'Reilly Media, 2009.

H

I

J

L

M

N

O

P

ABOUT THE AUTHOR

Robert Grayson, an award-winning former daily newspaper reporter, has written articles for numerous business publications and Web sites. His published pieces have profiled corporate leaders, as well as spotlighted the latest innovations, products, technology, marketing, and public relations trends in business, industry, and commerce. In addition, Grayson has written books for young adults.

PHOTO CREDITS

Cover (background, front and back), p. 1 © www.istockphoto.com/Andrey Prokhorov; cover (front inset) Francesco Ruggeri/Photographer's Choice/Getty Images; p. 7 © AP Images; p. 8 © Kent Meireis/The Image Works; p. 16 © Leilani Hu/Sacramento Bee/ZUMA Press; p. 19 © www.istockphoto.com/Pali Rao; p. 24 Tim Boyle/Getty Images; p. 26 Nikki Kahn/The Washington Post/Getty Images; p. 33 Patrik Jonsson/The Christian Science Monitor/Getty Images; p. 36 Melanie Burford/The Dallas Morning News/Newscom.com; p. 43 Sean Gallup/Getty Images; p. 47 Charlotte Southern/Bloomberg/Getty Images; p. 51 © Libby Volgyes/Palm Beach Post/ZUMA Press; p. 55 David Paul Morris/Bloomberg/Getty Images; p. 60 © John Gerhard; p. 64 Andre J. Jackson/Detroit Free Press/MCT/Newscom.com.

Designer: Matthew Cauli; Editor: Bethany Bryan; Photo Researcher: Amy Feinberg